ICK! YUCK! EEW!

OUR GROSS AMERICAN HISTORY

LOIS MINER HUEY

M MILLBROOK PRESS MINNEAPOLIS

For Paul—
HUSBAND, ARCHAEOLOGIST,
AND HISTORIAN EXTRAORDINAIRE

Many thanks to my critique group: Nancy, who urged me to write this, and Helen, Kyra, Liza, and Rose, who helped pull it together. Special thanks to Sally Walker for pointing me in the right direction, and to curators Robin and Joe for advice on clothing. And finally, I'd like to express appreciation to editor Carol Hinz for her interest and enthusiasm.

Milbrook Press
A division of Lerner Publishing Group, Inc.
241 First Avenue North
Minneapolis, MN 55401 U.S.A.

Website address: www.lernerbooks.com

Library of Congress Cataloging-in-Publication Data

Huey, Lois Miner.
    Ick! Yuck! Eew! : our gross American history / by Lois Miner Huey.
        pages   cm
    Includes bibliographical references and index.
    ISBN 978–0–7613–9091–6 (lib. bdg. : alk. paper)
    ISBN 978–1–4677–1710–6 (eBook)
    1. United States—History—Miscellanea—Juvenile literature. I. Title.
E178.3.H93 2014
973—dc23   2013004386

Manufactured in the United States of America
1 – BP – 7/15/13

CONTENTS

THE YUCKY PAST

HAVE YOU EVER WANTED TO TAKE A TRIP IN A TIME MACHINE? You'd set it for, say, 1770. You'd visit an early American city, ride a horse along cobblestone streets, go to a fancy ball, and grab a bite to eat.

North America in the 1700s wasn't all fun and fancy balls. Sometimes it could be downright disgusting.

THINK AGAIN.

What was life back then *really* like? Let's take a look at some of the gross things in the past—including smells, bugs, diseases, clothing, and hair. These alone will make you realize . . . you couldn't stand to be there.

You'll land in the month of June in a city populated mostly by white settlers. You'll meet wealthy people and middle-class folks. You probably won't spot any Native Americans there, but you'll see some black slaves who work as house servants and in shops. The slaves share many of the same yucky habits as their masters, of course.

You may notice a lot of things are not what you expected. Some of them might be upsetting. This was a time when black people were enslaved. People sometimes suffered greatly from diseases that we can now easily—and painlessly—cure. Other things may not be upsetting, but they sure will be gross! And that's what this journey is all about.

As a visitor from the future, you'll have the special ability to blend in as needed so that you don't call too much attention to yourself. People will be happy to talk with you, but they'll have no idea just how different from them you really are. So get ready for a whole lot of *ick*, *yuck*, and *eew*!

CHAPTER ONE

THE AWFUL SMELLS

HAVE YOU EVER VISITED A DUMP? Or been near the bear enclosure at the zoo on a hot day? Then you know icky smells.

America stank in the 1600s. And the 1700s. And the early 1800s.

SMELLY STREETS

Look! Lots of horses clomp down the street. They toss their heads and look pretty on one end. But at the other end, they poop. Cows roam the streets—and poop. Huge pigs run wild, eating garbage, which also stinks. The pigs poop. In New York City, the real streets haven't been seen in years. There's too much poop. The same is true everywhere—in cities, towns, and farms.

As shown in this 1827 print, dogs, pigs, horses, and other animals could be found stinking up the streets in New York City's Bowery neighborhood as well as countless other areas.

A Fine-Feathered Cleaning Crew

In Charleston, South Carolina, a large marketplace where people bought food often was filled with rotting leftovers. But luckily for residents, birds were on hand to clean up the mess. Buzzards regularly swooped down to grab pieces of meat and other food.

With their bald heads and sharp beaks, buzzards aren't very pretty. Even so, they provided a valuable service, so it was against the law to kill them. Unfortunately, because they ate rotten meat, the birds also stank. But at least they didn't fill the streets with a lot of poop!

Americans long ago had to be careful when emptying their chamber pots. They shouted out warnings, but sometimes visitors still got soiled.

And if the layers of poop weren't enough, dead dogs, cats, and rats pile up in the streets. The smell is awful on a hot summer day like today. No one bothers to pick up poop, dead animal bodies, or trash from the streets. Such conditions are just a part of life—and not the concern of the city government.

Sometimes human poop ends up in the streets too. People don't have indoor toilets so they keep containers called chamber pots under their beds to use, especially at night. These stink in the morning and need to be emptied. Sometimes the contents are tossed out the bedroom window onto the street below. Of course, a warning is called out first. But it doesn't always help.

In 1801 in York, Pennsylvania, a couple was walking down the street to go to a wedding. The contents of a chamber pot landed all over the woman, ruining her silk dress. At least she wasn't the bride!

SMELLY HOMES

After all the odors out on the streets have taken their toll, you head indoors to escape.

No luck.

The first floor of this small wooden house is a shoemaker's shop. The master welcomes you while his slave continues to pound nails into the soles of shoes. You can smell poop here too. It has come in from the street on the hems of customers' long skirts and clings to the boots of both men and women. The owner and his family live in the back of the shop. You sniff the air. You can tell that the bedroom chamber pots weren't emptied today.

The fireplace in the little kitchen behind the shop smokes, and the air makes you cough. And since a pot of stew cooks on that fireplace all day long, you can smell food burning too.

The family who lives here eats fresh meat, vegetables, and fruit in summer. Unfortunately, there is no refrigerator. So the food sits out, slowly rotting and filling the air with awful odors. But it'll be eaten anyway. **Yuck!**

How would you feel about skinning or plucking your dinner before cooking it every night?

SMELLY YARDS

You head to the backyard. Ah, a little better.

But the yard is a real mess. Oyster shells, small bones, broken dishes, and glass litter the dirt. You walk carefully to the back of the yard. Another smell hits you. Rotten food. You see seriously smelly garbage, including large, rotting animal bones, piled up on the ground.

Next, you arrive at an outdoor toilet. It's called the "necessary," the "privy," or the "outhouse." It's a small wooden structure with a door. Even if the smell doesn't tell you what it is, the flies buzzing around it do.

The necessary. The privy. The outhouse. The outdoor toilets of early America went by many names, but they all stank.

You put a cloth over your nose and open the door. It's dark inside. You see a wood shelf with two round holes cut through it. (Smaller privies had one hole.) Underneath is a deep pit, called a shaft, dug to hold the human waste that falls from above. No flush toilet, no running water.

Imagine doing your business here every day. It's hot, stinky, and buggy in summer, and it's freezing cold and dark in winter. There's no way to wash your hands afterward unless you stop at the well and pump some water. Most people don't make the effort. **Eew!**

Other Places to Pee

When men went to a party, they expected to be able to relieve themselves without going outside. So chamber pots sat in a corner or in a small cupboard for the men to use.

Farm families often didn't dig privies. Instead, they went behind nearby trees or bushes, as did farmers and plantation slaves. What about people in town who needed to go? They had to do their business in an alley. The alleys weren't cleaned either. Gross!

This pewter chamber pot dates back to the 1700s.

Skipping Bath Time

For hundreds of years, people thought bathing was harmful to their health. They believed a coating of dirt on the body kept out bad air that caused disease. Bathing also was a nuisance. Hauling water into the house, heating it in the fireplace, and pouring it into a tub—all too much work.

SMELLY PEOPLE

Remember those smelly bears at the zoo? When you enter a room filled with early Americans, the odor isn't all that different.

A French visitor reported that American women regularly wash their faces and hands. However, they seldom wash their feet and very seldom their bodies. Mothers make their children wash their faces and hands—or maybe not. Deodorant doesn't exist. Although men don't seem to care about body odor, rich ladies sometimes wear heavy perfumes to hide the smells.

In the 1700s and the 1800s, taking a bath was hard work. So wealthy women sometimes settled for hiding their foul odors. They used perfume, like the kind stored in this glass container from the nineteenth century.

You knock on the door of a house. A black woman servant invites you in. Your nose runs as you approach the people in a room.

When a woman smiles at you, you see she's missing several teeth. Her breath is horrid. You can't escape it. Almost everyone in the room has bad breath from rotting teeth. Plus, both men and women smoke white clay pipes. So their breath (and clothes and hair) also smells of strong tobacco.

People aren't completely unaware of the smells. They know they have bad breath. Women try to hide it by chewing cinnamon, cloves, orange peel, and honey melted in ashes. Men don't bother. Women mostly wave fans to keep the smell away and to cover their own black smiles.

Native American Bathing

Native Americans often took baths in creeks or sweated themselves clean in steam lodges. They found Europeans in large numbers very smelly. They also questioned why Europeans blew their noses into a fine handkerchief, folded it, and put it in a pocket. Was snot something worth keeping? they wondered. The Native Americans just threw their snot on the ground.

As shown in this 1883 image, many Americans long ago smoked clay pipes. At least the icky tobacco smell covered up the stink of their bad breath!

13

CHAPTER TWO

THE CREEPY-CRAWLY BUGS

BUGS HAVE ALWAYS BEEN WITH US, AND THEY ALWAYS WILL BE. But in early America, they were much more of a problem than they are now. If you had to give up modern methods of pest control, such as mosquito repellants and pesticides, you'd surely suffer!

BUZZING MOSQUITOES

It has been a long, stinky day, and you're ready for a good night's sleep. You check into a tavern that offers beds for rent. Unfortunately, you find out you'll have to share a bed with a man and a woman you don't know. The tavern is filled with smelly people and tobacco smoke, so you step outside. Immediately you're surrounded by hungry mosquitoes. You've never seen so many of them at once! You're just wearing a T-shirt and jeans, and you're soon covered with bites. You rush back inside only to find mosquitoes there too. So what can you do about these pests? Try putting live coals in dishes to keep them away. Or scorch (burn) brown sugar in bowls to smoke them out of rooms. **Stinky!**

Taverns

In addition to being a place where travelers stopped for the night, a tavern was where people gathered to drink and exchange news. Taverns were very common in cities. New York had 220 of them by 1756. More taverns were located in the countryside. Travelers could find them spaced apart about the distance of a typical day's journey by horseback or carriage.

Got a mosquito problem? Here's a hot tip: people in the 1700s and the 1800s burned brown sugar to keep the pests away.

This magazine illustration from the late 1800s gives an idea of just how troublesome mosquitoes were back in the days before pesticides.

Mosquitoes were a shock to newly arrived Europeans. There are no such insects on the other side of the Atlantic. One French priest told his countrymen back home, "The greatest torture of all is . . . the mosquitoes. I really believe that the plagues of Egypt were not more agonizing. This little animal has inspired more oaths [swear words] . . . than have been uttered in all the world until now."

You wonder how people stand these attacks, especially since you know something these people don't: mosquitoes spread disease. To the people you are watching, these bugs are just another bloodthirsty pest.

CREEPING BEDBUGS

Still itching, you climb the narrow wooden stairs to your room. The couple in the bed is already asleep, fully clothed. You push your way in. In the dark, you don't

see the little red bugs all over the bed. But as soon as you lie down, they attack your body. They bite and bite and bite some more. Each bite injects saliva that can cause swelling. You go crazy with itching. The bugs don't have wings, so they crawl everywhere: all over you, the bed, the wallpaper, and the floor. A single female can lay about five hundred eggs in her lifetime. Yuck and then some!

You get up and feel your way to an upholstered chair across the room. (There's no electricity, so nighttime is REALLY dark.) Ahh . . . you settle in to sleep. But wait. Bedbugs love upholstered furniture too. In fact, in most early American homes, such chairs are used only as seating for old people. And those chairs always seem to be home to any number of horrible biting bugs. You spend the night itching from the mosquitoes and the bedbugs, fidgeting, and wishing for dawn. You wonder how people in the past ever got any sleep.

Bed or parasite paradise? The answer is both. Like mosquitoes, bedbugs feed on blood— but unlike mosquitoes, European settlers brought these pests with them.

Unlike mosquitoes, bedbugs didn't exist in America until the Europeans brought them across the Atlantic in their baggage. So some people are used to them. But that didn't mean they are happy about it! In 1794 Albert Sanger of Keene, New Hampshire, took down his bed and carried the frame to the creek on his property. He pushed it entirely into the water, then soaked and scrubbed it. It didn't get the bugs out. In the early 1800s, Sarah Bryant of Cummington, Massachusetts, cooked her bed frame to rid it of bedbugs. This may have worked as the bugs can be killed by high temperatures.

When your visit here comes to an end, you'll need to be careful when you climb in your time machine. You'll want to be sure you don't bring any of those nasty bedbugs with you when you return to the present day. If you do, they'll hide in your clothes and wait for dark. Then they'll creep out and start biting again. Beware that you might find bedbugs in the twenty-first century as well. They are showing up in hotels, motels, and homes. They hitch rides in suitcases and clothes and spread from place to place. Getting rid of them without using strong poisons (which can be bad for the environment) is very difficult.

Modern pest controllers use extreme heat to treat bedbug infestations.

CRAWLING FOOD BUGS AND FLIES

You visit the kitchen of the tavern where you slept last night. The cook is pulling out items like flour and crackers. Before she begins to cook, she kills the insects crawling around in the food. You notice she misses some. Maybe this adds protein? **Gross!** You leave.

You walk down the street. You pass a butcher shop where slabs of meat are hanging for all to see. The meat is covered with bugs, especially flies. The butcher swishes away the flies as he cuts off pieces for customers. The buyers seem fine with it. **Eew!** Nope, you don't want to eat anywhere near there either.

Flour beetles *(above)* love to crawl around in, well, you guessed it. Discovering these critters was a common occurrence for cooks. At butcher shops *(right)*, flies were a bigger problem, even all the way into the early 1900s.

American flies were another shock to European settlers. Barn flies swarm into nearby houses. They crawl over people's faces and hands, over their food and drink, and over animals and furniture. One writer described a scene he witnessed in a Philadelphia home: "When a rather large room is suddenly opened in the summer, a noise is produced there which imitates that of the sea roaring in the distance; it is the flies who are escaping and cover you as they pass." **Ick!**

You finally sit down in another tavern to enjoy a meal served by a black slave. And the flies arrive. They especially enjoy the dessert, but they also seem to taste everything else they can find. **Yuck!**

Many people hang up sticky white paper to catch flies. This works, but so many flies get stuck to the paper that it soon gets all black and icky. It has to be changed often. Other people put out saucers of acid that kill the flies when they land in it. Either way, people are left with large numbers of dead flies. According to one traveler, "In large stores, dead flies must be swept up at least four times a day. They are gathered by bushels." The flies are then fed to chickens.

Flypaper took care of some winged pests. But people who didn't want dead insects for decoration had to change the strips of paper often.

BITING LICE

In early America, lice were everywhere. Like bedbugs, lice are small and wingless, and they bite and suck blood. They have specially developed claws that allow them to cling firmly to the hair where they lay their eggs. If you look carefully, you can see them in people's hair as well as lying in wait in bedding. Lice feed on blood several times a day. People infested with lice can feel them moving around on their heads. You notice people itching and scratching. The bugs' spit causes that reaction. **Ick!**

Is your scalp starting to itch? It might be head lice. These nasty wingless insects infested many a wig—and a head—in the 1700s and 1800s.

In the early 1700s, some men and women wear wigs, and lice infest those too. If women do wear their own hair, they pile it high on their heads and may add wig hair called extenders. At least once a week, they have to "open the head" of their own hair or their wigs to kill lice within. They use a fine-toothed comb to comb out the bugs and their eggs. Then they treat the hair with acids. This causes the scalp to burn, bringing tears to women's eyes. **Ouch!**

Some men shave their hair and tuck the wig over a bald head. This makes the lice easier to find, but it also makes the scalp more accessible to the bugs' bites. Often you see white lice crawling out from under a wig, ignored by the wig's wearer. **Gross!**

People treat lice by soaking bed linens in poisons. The poison left on the sheets will kill the lice, but it also can seep into the skin of whoever sleeps on them. **Yuck!**

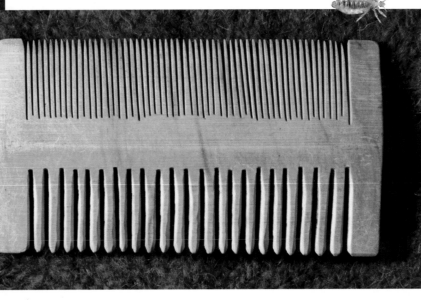

People turned to wigs and combs to help solve the lice problem, but no solution was perfect.

Bugs on the Inside

Not every bug can be seen with the eye. Some archeologists look in the ground for information about the past. They often find the shafts that once sat below privies. (The wooden structures above are long gone.) To study the people who used these long-forgotten privies, the archaeologists collect the rich soil inside and send it for testing. This reveals the eggs of bugs such as tapeworms and hookworms *(below)*. These bugs lived inside people in early America, and they passed through people's bodies and into the privy shafts. People didn't know about these bugs inside their bodies, but they suffered from fever, diarrhea, and even death as a result. These "hidden" bugs made people sick for thousands of years before effective treatments such as antibiotics were discovered.

CHAPTER THREE

THE NASTY GERMS

AFTER FINISHING YOUR FLY-INFESTED MEAL, YOU WANDER DOWN A CITY STREET. Then you stop and stare. People are crossing the street to avoid a house ahead of you. The road by the house is closed by fences at both ends. A flag is raised in front with the word *SMALLPOX* painted on it. What is going on?

PUS-FILLED POX

A woman carrying a laundry basket stops to explain the strange flag. The family that lives in the house shut themselves inside because they've been inoculated against the pox. To do this, a doctor makes a small slice in a person's arm until blood appears. The doctor then puts pus from another patient's smallpox blisters into the cut. **Eew!**

The family knew they would all still come down with smallpox but a lighter case of it than they would if they caught the disease in any other way. The woman explains that most people survive this procedure, and the family will emerge from the house in a few weeks. You imagine all those sick people with blisters filled with pus on faces, inside their mouths, and on the bottom of their feet and palms of their hands. Once the blisters break, they itch like crazy. **Ick!**

You remember seeing many people on the streets with scars on their faces. They must have survived a smallpox infection. You thank the woman and hurry away, as does everyone else who comes by this house.

A smallpox infection could cover a person's body with fluid-filled blisters.

Smallpox Basics

Smallpox is a disease caused by a virus. It has been completely wiped out since 1980, but it was very common in the world for thousands of years. Passed from person to person, it infected everyone from missionaries to housewives. After the first Europeans arrived in the Americas, bringing the disease with them, smallpox devastated Native American populations. But Europeans and African slaves were vulnerable to the disease as well. In one American outbreak from 1775 to 1782, one hundred thousand people died. Many more suffered from blindness and ugly scars. The introduction of inoculation led many wealthy and middle-class Americans to try it rather than take a chance on catching the disease otherwise. And once they had been through it, they were immune for life.

George Washington vs. Smallpox

In the early years of the American Revolution (1775–1783), smallpox swept through George Washington's Continental Army. With so many soldiers suffering from the disease, the Americans couldn't put up much of a fight against the British. Finally, Washington insisted that all his men be inoculated. Because inoculation was so risky, his decision was controversial, but it may have saved his army—and made it possible for the Americans to win the war.

TERRIBLE TEETH

Ahead of you in the street, you see a sign for a barber. Loud screams come from inside. Does someone need help?

You stop in the doorway, and your stomach heaves at the scene in front of you. A man is lying back in a chair, his arms and legs flailing about while the barber pulls a tooth from his wide-open mouth. He obviously had nothing to kill the pain before the barber began. Blood spurts out all over the patient and the barber. **Yuck!** Who knew barbers also were dentists?

People don't take good care of their teeth. If they clean their teeth at all, they do so with a finger or a twig. Bristle brushes are available but expensive. Plus, the bristles often break off or stick in the gums, causing more infection. Most people go through life with sunken cheeks, gaps from missing teeth, and frequent pain from cavities. **Ouch!**

Toothbrushes were available by the 1800s, but they weren't common. Not just anyone could afford this luxury item.

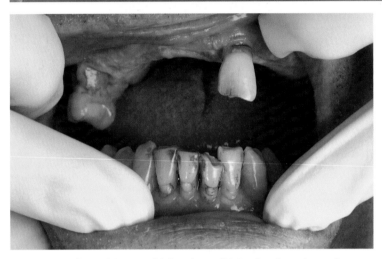

Missing teeth, cavities, and infections didn't give Americans long ago much to smile about. These dentures *(right)* made from lead, human teeth, cow teeth, and elephant ivory belonged to George Washington.

Barbers as Surgeons

Because of their skills with sharp instruments, barbers in early America sometimes performed operations. They removed arms, fingers, and other body parts when absolutely necessary. All without painkillers for their patients, except maybe alcohol. Ouch!

TORTUROUS TREATMENTS

If you'd been born in early America, your chances of living to the age of five would not have been good. Infections such as mumps, measles, scarlet fever, whooping cough—even chicken pox—threaten young lives. And there are no cures. A couple with four or five children will probably lose at least one to such diseases—and sometimes all of them at once, with sickness spreading from one child to another. Even if you made it past childhood, you still wouldn't have been safe. Dirt, bad water from polluted wells, poor diets, and accidents all contribute to adults dying young. People who survive childhood and avoid serious illness later in life might live into their sixties.

Keeping Josiah Quincy Strong

Parents tried to toughen up their children, believing the children would then have a better chance of surviving illness. Three-year-old Josiah Quincy was taken out of bed every morning, in warm or cold weather, carried down to the cellar, and dipped three times in cold water. Brr! He later grew up to become an important leader in the American Revolution.

Families large and small regularly lost children to diseases that most children today never experience, thanks to modern vaccines. This late nineteenth-century family has done well.

No one in early America knows about germs. You see a man carrying a black bag come out of a house. You ask him if he's a doctor. He pats you on the head and agrees to answer your questions. Why do people get sick? He says that sickness is caused by imbalances inside the body. He tries to cure illness and restore that balance by removing extra fluids. One of these fluids is blood. To remove blood, he cuts open a vein with a sharp knife and lets the blood flow into a bowl. When enough blood is collected, he believes balance is restored to the patient. If the patient stays sick, then he was wrong and more bloodletting is necessary. **Double yuck!**

Germs? What germs? Most people in early America believed sickness came from imbalances in the body—and one "cure" was bloodletting.

Bloodsucking worms are sometimes applied to the skin. They take out more blood. The patient has to lie still, watching the little brown leeches work on a body part. **Ick!** When the leeches have filled themselves with blood, they drop off. And when they're hungry again, they'll be used on another patient. **Eew!**

Bodily fluids besides blood may also need to be removed, the doctor says. Vomiting and pooping help clear the body too. So he gives patients large amounts of icky liquids or a plant called puke weed to cause violent discharges at both ends of the body. **Cramps! Mess! Gross!**

Bloodsucking Benefits

Leeches are still used in modern medicine. As yucky as this seems, the spit they put into the human body while sucking out blood is useful. It helps prevent blood clots from forming and helps restore blood flow to swollen areas. Leeches are especially helpful in cases where fingers, hands, toes, legs, and ears have been reattached.

Puke weed does just what you think it would do— makes you puke!

Another treatment involves putting a hot object—such as the rim of a glass jar or a fireplace poker—on the skin. Some doctors also used plasters spread with acid or lye. These remedies cause liquid-filled blisters to form. The doctor then breaks the blisters to release bodily fluids. **Pain! Scars! Eew!**

Once the right amount of blood, pus, vomit, poop, sweat, or urine is removed, the patient is cured. Or dead.

Which would you prefer on your skin: the rim of a hot glass jar or the tip of a heated fireplace poker?

CHAPTER FOUR

THE UNCOMFORTABLE FASHIONS

IT'S A WARM JUNE DAY, AND YOU'RE WORKING UP QUITE A SWEAT WITH ALL THE WALKING YOU'VE BEEN DOING. Thank goodness you don't have to wear much more than your jeans and a T-shirt.

But that's not the case for anyone else you've seen. People in the 1700s dress in layers of clothing year-round. And they don't just jump out of bed in the morning and quickly throw on their clothes. Oh, no. Getting dressed is a time-consuming task.

Males and females do not dress alike. Both wear plenty of uncomfortable garments, though. The one thing they all have in common is that no one wears underpants. **Yuck!** (Underpants don't become a regular part of the wardrobe until about 1850.)

GIRLS AND WOMEN

Girls and women wear a long loose undergarment called a shift next to their skin. Scoop-necked and short-sleeved, a shift hangs from the shoulder to above the ankles. It is worn all day and all night, again and again, until the next laundry day. Remember, people don't bathe regularly, so even a clean shift goes over a smelly body. **Ick!**

Families like this worked hard to look so stylish. Getting dressed could be a daily ordeal for Americans of all ages.

Over the shift comes a corset (also called stays). A corset consists of fabric lined with long pockets. Strips of bone are shoved down into the pockets to stiffen the fabric and help the wearer's posture. The corset is laced in the front. Corsets aren't used to hide fat but to force people to stand erect. Good posture is considered essential to good looks. Corsets aren't just for grown women either. Little girls, boys, and some men are laced up too, also to encourage good posture.

The rest of the clothing covers the corset: layers of petticoats (several slips) or one layer of a frame of hoops fastened together with tape, worn to spread out a woman's dress. Then comes the dress, usually called a gown. Finally is a neckerchief; an apron; a cap; and, for wealthier women, shoes with low heels. (Poor people go barefoot most of the time.) Shoes aren't made for left and right feet. Wearing the same shape on each foot is uncomfortable and awkward, to say the least. The same is true of boots worn by men and women outside the house. Sores and blisters are common. **Ouch!**

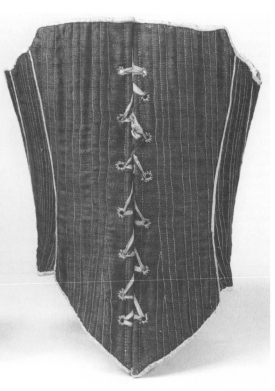

These corsets from the eighteenth century made sure their wearers stood up straight.

BOYS AND MEN

Boys and men also wear many layers. First comes a shirt worn day and night. The shirt sometimes has ruffles down the front and at the end of the sleeves. Its long tails are often crossed between the legs (remember, no underpants) and tucked into breeches. Lucky for men, these pants stop at the knees. Knee pants allow more freedom than women's skirts do.

The shirt collar is closed with a neck cloth, called a stock. A man folds it several times, wraps it around his neck, and ties a bow in front. He buttons a vest over the top of the shirt and then adds a coat. Stockings must be tied above the knee, but they're always coming loose and wrinkling. Men and boys often need to fix them. **Sigh!** That's a lot of clothing to wear in the middle of the summer.

Knee pants, neck cloths, ruffles, and breeches—no wonder the man below looks so grumpy. He spent all morning putting on these many impractical items of clothing.

WORKING PEOPLE AND CHILDREN

Shopkeepers, farmers, and servants dress more lightly, but they still wear more than one layer of clothes. And the clothes are covered with leather aprons. Women who work in shops, on farms, or as servants wear only a single petticoat under a simple gown. But these women still sometimes lace themselves into a kind of corset that holds them up straight.

Both little boys and little girls up to about the age of five are dressed in petticoats and dresses. That way, their diapers can easily be changed, and as they get older, they can use the toilet more easily.

You look down at your jeans, T-shirt, and sneakers. Things certainly have changed in the comfort department for lucky kids like you.

These shoemakers had a simple manner of dress compared to that of wealthier people in the mid-1800s.

LAUNDRY DAY

You stop by a house and watch the family doing laundry outdoors. Young boys haul buckets of water to tubs set out in the yard. One of them sees you and ambles over to say hello. The boy flexes his muscles and says he has to haul about 100 gallons (379 liters) of water each time laundry is done. **Wow!** That's at least two full bathtubs of water!

He explains that Ma makes her own soap. First, she pours water into a barrel with fireplace ashes and lime. This makes lye. Lye is a harsh chemical that can eat away a person's skin. **Eew!** Then Ma mixes the lye with animal fat and a little more lime powder. She boils it until a soft soap is left. That's a lot of work—and the washing hasn't even started!

Lime?

Lime is a white powder gotten by burning limestone, a common stone in America. It is used in laundry, in mortar and cement, and to sweeten the smells coming from privies.

At Silver Dollar City in Branson, Missouri, a modern craftsperson makes cakes of lye soap using the techniques of early Americans.

The boy adds that Ma washes only shifts, shirts, poopy diapers, bedsheets, and stockings. Outer clothing such as coats, breeches, vests, and gowns are almost never washed. Diapers that contain pee but no poop are not washed but just hung up to dry and then reused. **Gross!**

You watch Ma and the girls scrub and rub the clothes with soap and sometimes stale urine. The ammonia in urine helps cloth stay white. After they rinse the clothes, they lift the wet, heavy pieces into water boiling in a large brass pot over an outdoor fire. They stir the clothes with a stick. Then they lift out the clothes, scrub them some more, rinse them, and wring out the water. The clothes are smoothed

Forget washing machines and dryers. Laundry long ago involved brass pots, open flames, and a lot of physical labor.

out by hand and hung out to dry, usually on the grass or bushes. In winter or in rainy weather, the wet clothes go inside on a line near the fireplace or in the attic. Water spills on the floors and freezes, and makes walking dangerous. Clothes dry slowly inside, if at all.

STYLISH HAIR

If wealthy men and boys wear wigs for the sake of fashion, they are made of expensive human hair. However, wigs gradually become less popular by the 1780s. Younger men pull their own hair back into what they called a queue, or what we would call a pigtail. They decorate these with ribbons or enclose them in a fancy covering. Most older, workingmen like shopkeepers wear wigs made of horsehair, goat hair, wool, or plant fibers called tow.

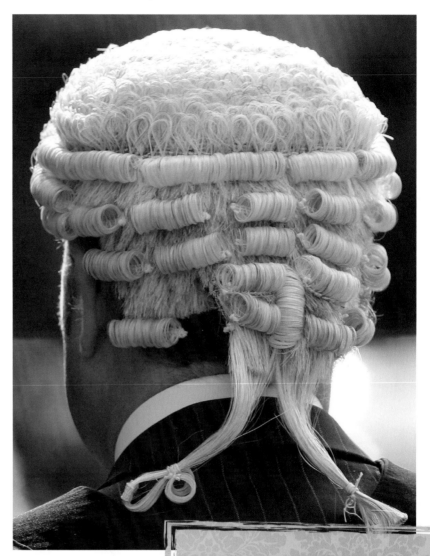

This judge in London, England, keeps an old tradition alive by sporting a wig for work.

Wigs in Court

Even today, judges and other court officials in the United Kingdom and in many other countries including Kenya and the Bahamas, wear white wigs in court. This is considered a tradition that adds dignity to court procedures.

Instead of wigs, many men choose to powder their own hair. People believe that white hair flatters the face, makes the eyes look brighter, and helps cover gray hairs. The process for powdering hair isn't pretty, though. A man applies grease to the hair to make the powder stick. The powder itself is flour or rice or wheat meal. A helper puts a special jacket over the man's shoulders. The man then holds a glass or paper cone over his face while powder flies all over the room. **_Achoo!_**

This cartoon from the mid-1700s has some fun with the practice of wig powdering.

The wealthy needed hours just to get dressed in the morning and fix their hair. And then they spent all day sweating under all those layers and worrying about keeping shoes and wigs from falling off. Men and women who have jobs to do don't have time for this. Their dress and hairstyles are simpler. Men wear pigtails, while women pile their hair up under a cap.

Powder Rooms

Rooms for applying powder to hair often were separate from bedrooms and dressing rooms in early America. The term *powder room* is still used in modern times. It generally refers to a small bathroom that has just a toilet and a sink.

Germs Are Good After All?

Surprisingly, our smelly, dirty past may have actually helped prevent some diseases. As Dr. Joel Weinstock from Tufts University in Massachusetts said, "If we all moved into a completely sterile [germfree] environment, we would die."

Doctors have noticed that certain conditions, including asthma and allergies, have increased as our surroundings have become less dirty. Better hygiene, cleaner water, and refrigeration mean fewer germs and fewer worms. People in the past routinely consumed worms (or their eggs) along with their water and food—or they picked up worms from the soil. Scientists have recently conducted a number of experiments in which people are swallowing pig whipworm eggs. (These eggs are normally found in pig intestines.) The eggs travel to the intestines, and larvae hatch from them. The larvae are harmless to humans, and the larvae leave the intestines before they develop into worms *(right)*. But while the larvae are in the body, they appear to affect the human immune system. These changes to the immune system may help reduce the occurrence of diseases that attack us from the inside, called autoimmune diseases.

Could you have tolerated going through all that day after day? You decide to get back home before someone tries to put colonial clothes on you. You hop into the time machine. You arrive home, relieved at returning to the good old twenty-first century. You've learned a lot about the past. And you begin to wonder how people in the future will view your time period. **Will they think it's yucky?**

Author's Note

Many historic sites are open to visitors. When you enter, you see green lawns and a well-painted house exterior. You seldom spot a privy structure or smell animal odors. Inside the buildings, all is clean. My research as an archaeologist—in which I dig historic sites as well as collect information found in diaries, journals, and newspapers—has given me a different view. I think that to understand history, people should be more aware of what these places really were like. In this book, I present a general picture of conditions in early America. There were exceptions, of course.

Much of the information presented in this book deals with wealthy and middle-class people. They were the writers and readers of their time, so the sources I used when researching this book had abundant information about them. But these people didn't write about everything. They rarely mention poopy streets or body odor. Visitors to early America do, though, so they were another good source for details about life in this era.

I didn't write about the grosser aspects of life long ago in order to make fun of early Americans. Instead, I wanted to paint a more accurate picture of how people lived. I don't think we should feel superior to the people of the past. They knew of nothing better than the conditions in which they lived. Despite all the hardships they faced, they worked hard, raised their children, and made the best of what they had.

GLOSSARY

acid: a chemical substance used for purposes such as killing insects and treating disease. A strong acid can burn the skin.

antibiotic: a medicine that kills bacteria and is used to treat infections and diseases. Antibiotics were not widely available until the twentieth century.

archaeologist: a scientist who studies evidence of ancient human, animal, and plant life. An archaeologist may dig up and examine old buildings, objects, and bones for information about the past.

ball: a formal gathering at which people dance and socialize

bloodletting: the opening of a vein for the purpose of removing blood. At one time, people believed that this practice could cure many diseases.

breeches: short pants that extend to just below the knee

buzzard: a large bird of prey with sharp claws

chamber pot: a pot into which a person could eliminate waste at night. These pots were used before there were indoor toilets.

cobblestone: a rounded stone of medium size, formerly used to pave streets

corset: a tight-fitting undergarment made from fabric and bone that was meant to improve posture. Women, children, and some men wore corsets.

extender: wig hair added to a person's natural hair to make it longer or fuller

hookworm: a parasitic worm that attaches itself to the intestines of a human or other animal host. It can make the host very sick.

hygiene: conditions and practices of cleanliness that promote good health of individuals and the community

infection: the presence and growth of bacteria or viruses in the body, which can result in disease

inoculate: to inject small amounts of a disease into a person's body to protect against the disease

lime: a white powder produced by heating limestone. It is used in fertilizer, mortar, and cement, and to reduce the strong smells that come from privies.

lye: a harsh chemical made from lime, fireplace ashes, and water. When mixed with animal fat, it makes soap.

pesticide: a substance used to kill pests such as insects, rodents, fungi, bacteria, and viruses

petticoat: a skirt or a slip that hangs from the shoulders or the waist and is worn under a dress

pollute: to damage or contaminate Earth, especially with waste produced by humans

privy: a small building (outhouse) without plumbing used as a toilet

shaft: the pit beneath a privy that catches human waste

shift: a scoop-necked, short-sleeved undergarment worn by women. It went under the corset and extended from the shoulders to just above the ankles.

smallpox: a contagious, sometimes deadly disease caused by a virus. It is characterized by a rash, high fever, and blisters.

stock: a wide band or a scarf that a man wore around his neck to keep his shirt collar closed

tapeworm: a parasitic worm that lives and lays its eggs inside the intestines of a human or other animal host. Many infected people have no symptoms, but in some cases, a tapeworm infection can make the host very sick.

tavern: a place where travelers can spend the night. Taverns were also places for people to gather to drink alcohol and exchange news.

upholstered: furniture that has been covered with materials such as fabric and padding

virus: an infectious agent that enters the body, causing infection or disease

Source Notes

16 Paul Poisson, quote from his journal as presented on a sign in an exhibit at Fort de Chartres, Illinois, photographed by the author.

20 Moreau de Saint-Méry, *Moreau de St. Méry's American Journey* (1793–1798), trans. Kenneth Roberts and Anna M. Roberts (Garden City, NY: Doubleday & Co., 1947), 325.

20 Ibid., 324.

41 Marni Jameson, "Here, Swallow This Worm: Novel Treatment Offers Hope to Those with Immune Diseases, Such as Crohn's," *Orlando Sentinel*, September 29, 2011, http://articles .orlandosentinel.com/2011-09-29/health/os-worm-treatment-20110927_1 _worm-therapy-crohn-inflammatory-bowel (March 21, 2013).

Selected Bibliography

Ashenburg, Katherine. *The Dirt on Clean: An Unsanitized History*. New York: North Point Press, 2007.

Bryson, Bill. *At Home: A Short History of Private Life*. New York: Doubleday, 2010.

Ewing, Elizabeth. *Dress and Undress: A History of Women's Underwear*. New York: Drama Book Specialists, 1978.

Fenn, Elizabeth A. *Pox Americana: The Great Smallpox Epidemic of 1775–82*. New York: Hill and Wang, 2001.

Fisher, Charles, Karl Reinhard, Matthew Kirk, and Justin DeVirgilio. "Prives and Parasites: The Archaeology of Health Conditions in Albany, New York." *Historic Archaeology* 41, no. 4 (2007): 172–197.

Garrett, Elizabeth Donaghy. *At Home: The American Family, 1750–1870*. New York: H. N. Abrams, 1990.

Hawke, David Freeman. *Everyday Life in Early America*. New York: Harper & Row, 1988.

Larkin, Jack. *The Reshaping of Everyday Life 1790–1840*. New York: Harper & Row, 1988.

Nylander, Jane C. *Our Own Snug Fireside: Images of the New England Home, 1760–1860*. New York: Alfred A. Knopf, 1993.

Saint-Méry, Moreau de. *Moreau de St. Méry's American Journey (1793–1798)*. Translated by Kenneth Roberts and Anna M. Roberts. Garden City, NY: Doubleday & Co., 1947.

Theobald, Mary Miley. *Death by Petticoat: American History Myths Debunked*. Kansas City, MO: Andrews McMeel, 2012.

Wright, Merideth. *Everyday Dress of Rural America, 1783–1800: With Instructions and Patterns*. New York: Dover Publications, 1992.

FURTHER READING

Books

Albee, Sarah. *Poop Happened! A History of the World from the Bottom Up.* New York: Walker Children's, 2010. Follow the habits of sanitation throughout human history. From plague outbreaks to important inventions and discoveries, it certainly has come a long way!

Beccia, Carlyn. *I Feel Better with a Frog in My Throat: History's Strangest Cures.* Boston: Houghton Mifflin, 2010. Read about unusual treatments for common ailments, and find out the science behind whether cures from a mother's kiss to leeches actually work.

Boyer, Crispin. *That's Gross! Icky Facts That Will Test Your Gross-Out Factor.* Washington, DC: National Geographic Children's Books, 2012. Learn about the history and science of all things gross in this engrossing read.

Davies, Nicola. *What's Eating You? Parasites—The Inside Story.* Cambridge, MA: Candlewick, 2009. Parasites are everywhere. Learn about their gross habits that help them live off other animals (and humans!) and how their hosts respond.

Kalman, Bobbie. *18th Century Clothing.* New York: Crabtree Publishing Co., 1993. Take a closer look at the many layers of clothes children and adults in America wore in the 1700s.

Masoff, Joy. *Oh, Yikes! History's Grossest Moments.* New York: Workman Publishing Company, 2006. Pick up this handy encyclopedia to learn about history's grossest moments, complete with photos, illustrations, and hands-on activities.

Websites

Colonial House—Interactive History
http://www.pbs.org/wnet/colonialhouse/history/index.html
Check out information about the American colonies in 1628, and take a "Would You Have Survived in the Colony?" quiz.

Colonial Life in Early America
http://www.kidinfo.com/american_history/colonization_colonial_life.html
This site has links to information about everything from black history and economics to clothing and music in colonial America.

Colonial Williamsburg—History for Kids
http://www.history.org/kids/index.cfm
Learn about daily life in colonial Williamsburg with activities, games, pictures, facts, and more.

Old Sturbridge Village—Kid Zone
http://www.osv.org/kids_zone/index.html
This site has interactive features such as crosswords, games, and a quiz. Learn about colonial tools, sayings, entertainment, and more. It also features a Q&A with a historian.

Places to Visit

Can't get enough of history? Check out these historic sites, either in person or online:

Colonial Williamsburg, Williamsburg, VA, http://colonialwilliamsburg.com

Morristown Battlefield, Morristown, NJ, http://www.nps.gov/morr

Mount Vernon, Alexandria, VA, http://www.mountvernon.org

Mütter Museum, Philadelphia, PA, http://www.collegeofphysicians.org/mutter-museum/

National Museum of Health and Medicine, Silver Spring, MD, http://www.medicalmuseum.mil/

Old Salem, Winston-Salem, NC, http://oldsalem.org

Smithsonian National Museum of American History, Washington, DC, http://americanhistory.si.edu

Valley Forge Battlefield, King of Prussia, PA, http://www.nps.gov/vafo/index.htm

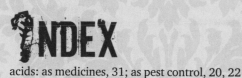

INDEX

Photo Acknowledgments

The images in this book are used with the permission of: © Miramisska/Dreamstime.com (vintage background); © Myszka50/Dreamstime.com (grunge vintage background); © iStockphoto.com/subjug, (round frame); © iStockphoto.com/Adam Korzekwa, (square frame); © Melinda Fawver/Dreamstime.com (beetle); © MorganOliver/Dreamstime.com (bedbug); © Vinicius Tupinamba/Dreamstime.com (mosquito); © Brandon Alms/Dreamstime.com (fly); Centers for Disease Control and Prevention Public Health Image Library/James Gathany (louse); © szefei/Shutterstock.com (leech); © SuperStock, pp. 4-5; © Bettmann/CORBIS, pp. 6-7, 13, 29; © Mary Evans Picture Library/Alamy, p. 8; © Leon Reding (19th Century)/The Art Gallery Collection/Alamy, p. 9; © Bill Brooks/Alamy, p. 10; © Museum of London/The Image Works, p. 11; © DEA/A. Dagli Orti/De Agostini/Getty Images, p. 12; © Mirceax/Dreamstime.com, p. 15; © Archive Photos/Stringer/Getty Images, p. 16; © Education Images/Universal Images Group/Getty Images, p. 17; © Justin Sullivan/Getty Images, p. 18; © Yap Kee Chan/Dreamstime.com, p. 19 (top); © Minden Pictures/SuperStock, p. 19 (middle); © Mary Evans Picture Library/Alamy, p. 19 (bottom); © Joel Sartore/National Geographic/Getty Images, p. 20; © Kallista Images/Getty Images, p. 21; © Huntington Library/SuperStock, p. 22 (left); © Jack Sullivan/Alamy, p. 22 (right); © Science Picture Co/Science Faction/SuperStock, p. 23; © Universal Images Group/SuperStock, pp. 24-25; © SSPL/Getty Images, p. 27 (top); © 1exposure/Alamy, p. 27 (middle left); © Glenn Stubbe/Minneapolis Star Tribune/CORBIS, p. 27 (middle right); © Classic Image/Alamy, p. 27 (bottom); The Granger Collection, New York, pp. 28, 34 (left); © Ivonne Wierink/Shutterstock.com, p. 30 (right); © Raia/Dreamstime.com, p. 31 (top); © Alexlukin/Dreamstime.com, p. 31 (bottom); © Geoffrey Clements/CORBIS, pp. 32-33; © Richard T. Nowitz/CORBIS, p. 34 (right); © Christie's Images/CORBIS, p. 35; © Everett Collection/SuperStock, p. 36; © Ted Streshinsky/CORBIS, p. 37; © Hulton Archive/Stringer/Getty Images, p. 38; © Peter Macdiarmid/Getty Images, p. 39; © Hulton Archive/Getty Images, p. 40 (left); © CNRI/Science Source, p. 41.

Front cover: © Burstein Collection/CORBIS (main); © Melinda Fawver/Dreamstime.com (long horned beetle); © MorganOliver/Dreamstime.com (bed bug); © szefei/Shutterstock.com (leech); © Miramisska/Dreamstime.com (background).

Back cover: © szefei/Shutterstock.com (leech); © Myszka50/Dreamstime.com (background).

Main body text set in Charter ITC Std Regular 13/18. Typeface provided by International Typeface Corporation.